A special gift for you

To

_____

From

_____

Introduction

Two friends were walking through a desert area. As they walked, they conversed about various topics. It was over a point of discussion that really didn't matter very much that they had an argument. The argument grew heated, and ended when one slapped the other one in the face. The one who got slapped was deeply hurt, but without saying anything, he wrote in the sand: "Today my best friend slapped me in the face."

They kept walking for a long time until they came upon an oasis, where they stopped to cool themselves in the water. The one who had been slapped went too far from the edge of the pool and became stuck in the mire. He struggled to get free, and began sinking. He would have drowned had not his friend saved him. After he recovered from the near drowning, he wrote on a stone: "Today my best friend saved my life."

The one who had first slapped and then later rescued his best friend asked him, "After I hurt you, you wrote in the sand, but now you write on a stone; why?"

The friend replied, "When someone hurts us we should write it down in sand where winds of forgiveness can erase it away. But, when someone does something good for us, we must engrave it in stone where no wind can ever erase it."

"when your face is dirty."

— Sicilian Proverb

A man that hath friends
must shew himself friendly:
and there is a friend that
sticketh closer than a
brother.

— King Solomon

"When I go to a beauty parlor I always enter through the

EMERGENCY

EXIT."

— *Phyllis Diller*

Then she said, Let me find favor in thy sight, my lord;
for that thou hast comforted me, and for that thou
hast spoken kindly unto thy handmaid . . . . — Ruth 2:13

"A friend is someone who

DANCES WITH YOU

in the sunlight and

WALKS BESIDE YOU

in the shadows."

— *Unknown*

And shout for joy, all ye that are upright in heart. — King David

"Those who bring

SUNSHINE to the lives of others CANNOT KEEP IT from themselves."

— Sir James M. Barrie

These things have I spoken unto you, that in me ye may have peace. In the world ye have tribulation: but be of good cheer; I have overcome the world. — John 16:33

"A friend is somebody

YOU WANT TO BE AROUND

when you feel like being

BY YOURSELF."

— *Barbara Burrow*

As in water face answereth to face, So the heart of man to man. — Prov. 27:19

"And all thy children shall be taught of Jehovah; and great shall be the peace of thy children." — Isa. 54:13

"It's NOT

WHERE you go,

or WHAT you do;

it's WHO
you take along with you."
— Unknown

"**VIRTUE** is the *safest helmet*."

— Motto of the sixteenth-
century ship, The Golden Hind

And take the helmet of salvation,
and the sword of the Spirit, which
is the word of God ....

— Eph. 6:17

"REAL FRIENDS

are those who, when

you've made a fool of

yourself, don't feel

that you've done a

PERMANENT

job."

— *Erwin T. Randall*

But the very hairs of your head are all
numbered. — Matt. 10:30

"WHEREVER
you are,

it is your

F R I E N D S

who make

your world."

— William James

Restore unto me the joy of thy salvation; And uphold me with thy free spirit. — King David

"What brings  to the

heart is not so much the friend's

gift as *THE FRIEND'S*

LOVE."

— St. Alfred of Rievaulx

Make no friendship with an angry man.
— King Solomon

"A
TRUE
FRIEND

But he that shall endure unto
the end, the same shall be
saved. — Mark 13:13

is someone who thinks you are a

GOOD EGG

even though he knows that you are

SLIGHTLY CRACKED."

— Bernard Meltzer

"Who finds a
FAITHFUL
FRIEND,

finds a

TREASURE."

— Jewish Saying

But there is a friend that sticketh closer than a brother.
— King Solomon

"ONE JOY dispels a HUNDRED cares."

— *Chinese Proverb*

And if I bestow all my goods to feed the poor, and if I give my body to be burned, but have not love, it profiteth me nothing. — I Cor. 13:3

If thou hast run with the footmen, and they have wearied thee, then how canst thou contend with horses?

— Jer. 12:5

"The road to a friend's house is *NEVER LONG.*"

— *Danish Proverb*

"Give me **ONE** friend

JUST ONE,

who meets the needs of

all my *VARYING*

MOODS."

— *Esther M. Clark*

BLESSED ARE THE PEACEMAKERS:

for they shall be called the children of God. — Matt. 5:9

"A SINGLE
ROSE can

be my garden ...

a single *friend,*

M Y WORLD."

— *Leo Buscaglia*

And he made of one blood all nations
of men for to dwell on all the face of
the earth. — Acts 17:26

"AGE

IS **NOT** IMPORTANT —

unless
you're a cheese."

— *Anonymous*

*Remember now thy Creator in the
days of thy youth, while the evil days
come not, nor the years draw nigh …*
— King Solomon

*Mercy and truth are met together;
Righteousness and peace have
kissed each other.* — King David

"A TRUE FRIEND is ONE SOUL in two bodies."

— *Unknown*

"With

M E R R Y

C O M P A N Y,

the dreary way is

endured."

— *Spanish Proverb*

*Sing, O heavens: and be joyful, O earth; and
break forth into singing . . . .* — Isa. 49:13

"Remember,

THE GREATEST
G I F T

is not found in a store nor

under a tree,

but in the *HEARTS*
of true friends."

— *Cindy Lew*

Wherefore let him that thinketh he standeth
take heed lest he fall. — 1 Cor. 10:12

"How
RARE